BOOKS BY
JUDITH VIORST

Poems

The Village Square
It's Hard to Be Hip Over Thirty and Other Tragedies of Married Life
People and Other Aggravations
How Did I Get to Be Forty and Other Atrocities
When Did I Stop Being Twenty and Other Injustices

Children's Books

Sunday Morning
I'll Fix Anthony
Try It Again, Sam
The Tenth Good Thing About Barney
Alexander and the Terrible, Horrible, No Good, Very Bad Day
My Mama Says There Aren't Any Zombies, Ghosts, Vampires,
    Creatures, Demons, Monsters, Fiends, Goblins, or Things
Rosie and Michael
Alexander, Who Used to Be Rich Last Sunday
If I Were in Charge of the World and Other Worries
The Good-Bye Book
Earrings!
The Alphabet from Z to A (with much confusion on the way)
Sad Underwear and Other Complications
Alexander, Who's Not (Do You Hear Me? I Mean It!) Going to Move

Other

Yes, Married
A Visit from St. Nicholas (to a Liberated Household)
Love and Guilt and the Meaning of Life, Etc.
Necessary Losses
Murdering Mr. Monti

FOREVER FIFTY

and Other Negotiations
by
JUDITH VIORST

Simon & Schuster

again, for Milton

SIMON & SCHUSTER
Rockefeller Center
1230 Avenue of the Americas
New York, New York 10020

Manufactured in the United States of America

9   10   8

Library of Congress Cataloging-in-Publication data
Viorst, Judith.
Forever fifty and other negotiations / by Judith Viorst;
illustrated by John Alcorn.
p.   cm.
1. Middle age—Poetry.   2. Aging—Poetry.   I. Title.
PS3572.I6F6   1989
811'.54—dc19

ISBN 0-684-83237-2   89-6412
CIP

Contents

FIFTY

You Say You Want to Know How Old I Am?   10
You Say You Want to Know How the Children Are Doing?   12
Wild Thing   14
Exercising Options   16
Postmortems   18
Confusion   20
To a Middle-Aged Friend Considering Adultery with a
      Younger Man   22
Happiness   24

STILL FIFTY

By My Age   28
Second Marriage   30
Brief Encounter at the Delicatessen   32
They're Back   34
Christmas Presents for Fifty Years and Over   36
And Now You Want to Know If There Is Anything Good to
      Say about Getting Older   38
Eight Basic Facts about Memory   40
How Can People Want to Bring Children into This Terrible
      World?   42

FOREVER FIFTY

Before I Go   46
You Might As Well Laugh   48
Some Advice from a Mother to Her Married Son   50
When Asked to What They Owe the Success of Their Marriage,
      He and She Completely Agree that Love Is Accommodation   52
Medical Tests   54
More Questions   56
A Sexy Old Lady   58
The Pleasures of an Ordinary Life   60

FIFTY

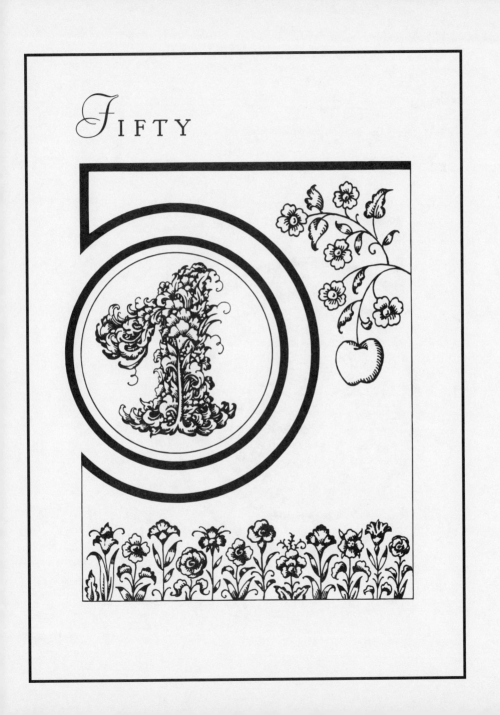

You Say You
Want to Know
How Old I Am?

I don't mind telling my age. I
	honestly don't mind telling my age.
But why are you asking?

I don't pretend I'm still young. I
	don't expect to be thought of as young.
So why are you asking?

I never lie about age. It's
	undignified to lie about age.
But why are you asking?

We're only as old as we feel. You
	know we're only as old as we feel.
So why are you asking?

I'm told I look good for my age. I'm
	often told I look good for my age.
Now why are you asking?

No, I'm not ashamed of my age. And
	if you insist, I'll tell you my age.
You're what? Still asking?

You Say You Want to Know How the Children Are Doing?

Shawn teaches wind-surfing. Dawn is a certified midwife.
Kim has converted from atheist to Bahai.
Justin has finally fallen in love with a practically
    perfect person,
Except he's a guy.

Holly quit teaching first grade to go into arbitrage.
Keith runs a health club and Kyle's a computer whiz.
Robin, who's on her second divorce and fourth therapist, feels
    that she's starting
To learn who she is.

Brandon has dropped out of medical school to write screenplays.
Josh has abjured material wealth to do good.
Kirsten and Stacy and Maya and Tracy have opted for
    partnership track
Over motherhood.

Andrea is a professional acupuncturist.
Damian's making a killing in real estate.
Tara has already given birth to Rebecca and Joseph and Jacob,
And plans to have eight.

Kevin has given up socks and acquired two earrings.
Devon has given up sweets and eats nothing impure.
And so, if you want to know how the children are doing,
The answer is,
We're not exactly sure.

Wild Thing

I went for a walk in the sun without wearing my sunscreen.
I went out of town without making a reservation.
I placed my mouth directly upon a public drinking fountain,
    and took a sip.
I didn't bother flossing my teeth before bedtime.
I pumped my own gasoline at a self-service station.
I ate the deviled egg instead of the cauliflower with low-fat
    yoghurt dip.
I bought, without reading *Consumer Reports*, a new dryer.
I left my checking account unreconciled.
I know that the consequences could be dire,
But sometimes a woman simply has to run wild.

Exercising Options

I've been told that the vigorous moving-about of my body
Could discourage all ills from loose flesh to a heart attack.
But there isn't a fitness routine
That strikes me as anything less than obscene, so
I float on my back.

I respect those brave ladies who're burning their flab off
    with Fonda.
They still wear bikinis. I long ago switched to a sack.
But my horror of thickening thighs
Is surpassed by my horror of exercise, so
I float on my back.

I admire all those stalwarts out jogging in blizzards and heat
    waves
But if I want torture, I'd just as soon head for the rack.
Let my upper arms droop, I aspire
To no exertion that makes me perspire, so
I float on my back.

And I know that I richly deserve the whole world's condemnation
For the firmness that both my torso and character lack.
Yes, my body's a total disgrace
But there is this big happy smile on my face as
I float on my back.

Postmortems

On the way home with my husband from the dinner party,
I thought I'd very tactfully point out
That he shouldn't interrupt, and that
He shouldn't talk with his hands, and that
He shouldn't, when discussing politics, shout.
And that he shouldn't tell that story while people
are eating, and that
He shouldn't tell that joke for the rest of his
life, and that
He shouldn't have said what he said about that
terrible lady in red because
She happens to be the-person-he-said-it-to's wife.
And that he didn't need that second helping of
mousse cake, and that
He didn't need to finish the Chardonnay.
But after thirty years of marriage
I finally understand what not to say
On the way home with my husband from a
dinner party.

Confusion

I can't figure out if it's gas or a coronary.
I can't figure out if it's hostile or benign.
I can't figure out if I'm turning into a hypochondriac,
    or just being sensible.
I can't figure out when we stop supporting our children.
(At twenty-one? At thirty? Forty-nine?)
I can't figure out if not bothering to change the sheets in the
    guest room in between houseguests is ever an option, or
    always reprehensible.

I can't figure out why men won't ask for directions.
(Is this genetic or could they be retrained?)
I can't figure out, when dressed in the height of fashion, if
    I'm looking incredibly chic or slightly ridiculous.
I can't figure out if my tale is enthralling or boring.
(What are those facial expressions? Spellbound? Or pained?)
I can't figure out if wanting all the hangers in my closet to
    face the same way means I'm obsessive-compulsive, or
    merely meticulous.

I can't figure out if I've gone from stable to stodgy.
(Is "reliable" what I want as my epitaph?)
I can't figure out if helping yourself to a shrimp from your
    spouse's plate ought to be viewed as intimacy or intrusion.
I can't figure out if I've lost my sense of humor
Or if, after fifty, it just gets harder to laugh.
And I can't figure out if everyone else has figured everything
    out, or whether we are all in a state of confusion.

To a Middle-Aged Friend Considering Adultery with a Younger Man

It's hard to be devil-may-care
When there are pleats in your derrière
And it's time to expose what your panty hose
    are concealing.
And although a husband's fond eyes
Make certain allowances for your thighs,
Young lovers might look less benignly at what
    you're revealing.

It's hard to surrender to sin
While trying to hold your stomach in
And hoping your blusher's still brightening up
    your complexion,
And hoping he isn't aware
As he runs his fingers through your dark hair,
That you've grown unmistakably gray in a whole
    other section.

It's hard to experience bliss
When sinus intrudes on every kiss
And when, in the tricky positions, your back
    starts to hurt you.
And when you add all it entails
To teach him what turns you on and what fails,
You might want to reconsider the virtues of
    virtue.

Happiness

(RECONSIDERED)

*H*appiness
Is a clean bill of health from the doctor,
And the kids shouldn't move back home for
        more than a year,
And not being audited, overdrawn, in Wilkes-Barre,
        in a lawsuit or in traction.

Happiness
Is falling asleep without Valium,
And having two breasts to put in my brassiere,
And not (yet) needing to get my blood pressure lowered,
        my eyelids raised or a second opinion.

And on Saturday nights
When my husband and I have rented
Something with Fred Astaire for the VCR,
And we're sitting around in our robes discussing
The state of the world, back exercises, our Keoghs,
And whether to fix the transmission or buy a new car,
And we're eating a pint of rum-raisin ice cream
        on the grounds that
Tomorrow we're starting a diet of fish, fruit and grain,
And my dad's in Miami dating a very nice widow,
And no one we love is in serious trouble or pain,
And our bringing-up-baby days are far behind us,
But our senior-citizen days have not begun,
It's not what I called happiness
When I was twenty-one,
But it's turning out to be
What happiness is.

STILL FIFTY

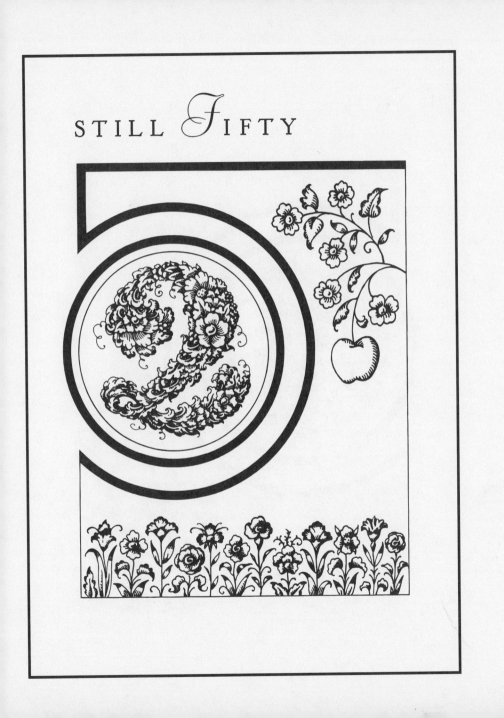

By My Age

By my age I thought I would finally be able to
Finish *Moby Dick*,
Wait for the meal to be served without eating the roll,
And display unruffled composure when I'm at a cocktail party
   where I don't know a single soul
And nobody talks to me,
Instead of wanting to run and hide in the bathroom.

By my age I thought I would finally be able to
Read a tax return,
Admit that I'm wrong when I'm wrong—and not gloat
   when I'm right,
And display serene acceptance when I watch my married son
   walk out into the cold and snowy night
In a pair of torn sneakers
Instead of screaming, Stop! You'll catch pneumonia.

By my age I thought I would finally be able to
Speak coherent French,
Refrain from providing advice unless someone begs,
And display mature detachment when this lady M.B.A. with
   perfect skin and even better legs
Makes a play for my husband,
Instead of plotting to push her face in the pasta.

By my age I thought I would finally be able to
Cope with Celsius,
Drive to New Jersey without getting lost every time,
And display a mature and serene and composed and detached
   and unruffled acceptance of all that I'm
Still not able to do
By my age.

Second Marriage

*H*e is a recent widower, very eligible.
She is a recent widow, attractive and bright.
And after several wonderful evenings together, they
    have decided that they are
Right for each other.

So as soon as their CPAs have reworked their tax structure,
And their doctors have pronounced them physically fit,
And their lawyers have found a formula for an equitable
    pre-nuptial agreement,
They intend to get married.

And he'll sell his condo in Aspen because she hates skiing.
And she'll sell her house at the beach because he hates sand.
And they'll merge their books and their records and their
    paintings and their furniture and
Their families:

His son who, at thirty, is having a spiritual crisis.
Her son who, at thirty, still hasn't started to date.
His daughter, who is deciding between becoming a single parent
    and going to business school.
Her daughter, who wants to know if they are planning, when they
    die, to be buried next to their first or their second mate.
His brother, who thinks he should have picked somebody younger.
Her sister, who thinks his taste in jackets is crude.
Her father, who has a lot to say about why Ronald Reagan was one
    of our greatest presidents.
Her mother, who has a lot to say about fiber and digestion
    and why a person should never eat fried food.
His aunt, who only hopes he knows what he's doing.
Her uncle, who is either having a major nervous breakdown
    or being followed by the CIA.
Her aunt, who talks about Charles and Diana as if—though she
    actually doesn't—she actually knows them.
His uncle, who talks with his mouth full because—he explains—if
    he waits till he's done, he always forgets what it is he intended
    to say.
Her cousin, who wants to sell them more life insurance.
His cousin, who wants to sell them some tax-free bonds.

And as soon as their therapists help them feel just a
Little bit fonder of each other's families,
They intend to get married.

Brief Encounter
at the
Delicatessen

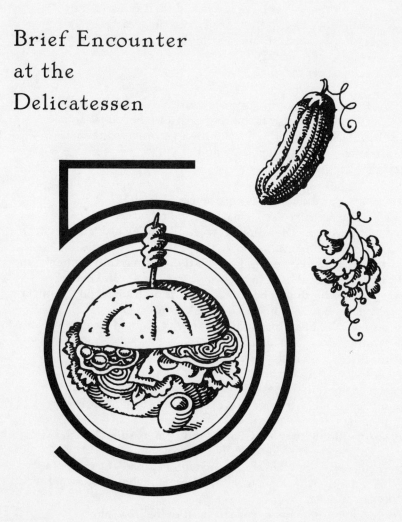

$\mathcal{S}$he has no muscle tone. He has no hair.
But when they meet beside the deli case,
Some force within their blood begins to race.
He orders half a pound of roast beef, rare,
Plus one pound each of corned beef and of tongue,
Along with coleslaw and a rye with seeds.
(Do married middle-agers have no needs?)
(Is untamed passion only for the young?)
His heart beats fast. Her thoughts are most unclean.
But mad desire yields to law and will.
She buys three whitefish and six pickles, dill,
Plus half a pound of hot pastrami, lean.

Then silently they part as (sigh) they must,
Surrendering to brunch instead of lust.

They're Back

When our last child left home we were terribly sad and dejected.
We were done with our parenting duties and felt disconnected.
We missed all the children, of course, but we fully expected
They would thrive in the world and live happily ever after.

When our last child left home we were terribly sad—for a minute.
But a whole new life beckoned, and we were prepared to begin it.
We planned for a glorious future with no children in it.
Let them thrive and do well and live happily ever after.

Our last child was gone for a month when we started receiving
Bad news from the eldest. Her marriage was through. She was
    leaving.
And soon she moved back to her room to do yoga and weaving,
And to blame us for not living happily ever after.

Then our middle son called us, collect, to announce he was
    yearning
To go back to school for another degree. He'd be earning
No money, and therefore was counting a lot on returning.
He's in his room studying happily ever after.

Our youngest got married and found that he couldn't afford her.
And so he reminded us how very much we adored her,
Then asked if we wouldn't be willing to bed and to board her.
They're both in his room loving happily ever after.

When our last child left home we felt sad, but we rapidly mended.
Now the children are back, and the future we started has ended.
The hot water runs out routinely. We hadn't intended
For six to be showering happily ever after.

Our children are home and too old to be told, Wear galoshes.
But too young, it seems, to wash dishes, for nobody washes,
Though they finish a week's worth of food in just one evening's
    noshes.
Yes, they're sitting around eating happily ever after.

Our children are home and we can't find the scissors or car keys.
There are sweat socks all over the living room. Whose the hell
    are these?
Each night we gaze up at the sky and we wish on a star: Please
Let them go somewhere else and live happily ever after.

Christmas Presents
for Fifty Years
and Over

He used to buy her lacy negligees.
She used to buy him jaunty turtlenecks.
But now they've moved into another phase:
More osteoporosis and less sex.

More Perrier, less Gevrey-Chambertin.
No sleeping—unawakened—through the night.
No cigarettes. No eggs. No beef. No tan.
And no, without bifocals, unblurred sight.

When Christmas comes, as it's about to come,
On what then do they plan to spend their dimes?
He's bought a pillbox for her calcium.
She's ordered him the large-type *New York Times*.

And Now You Want to Know If There Is Anything Good to Say about Getting Older

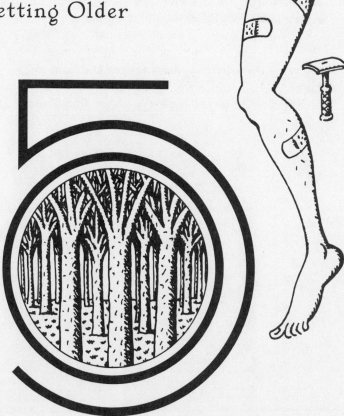

We aren't as self-centered as we used to be.
We're not as self-pitying—or as just plain dumb.
Middle age has come, and we find
(Along with the inability to sleep all night without
     a trip to the bathroom)
A few compensations.

We aren't as uncertain as we used to be.
We've learned to tell the real from the tinsel and fluff.
Getting old is tough, but we find
(Along with the inability to shave our legs unless
     we're wearing our glasses)
A few compensations.

We aren't as compliant as we used to be.
We choose our own oughts and musts and got-to's and shoulds.
We're deep into the woods, yet we find
(Along with the inability to eat a pepperoni pizza at
     bedtime)
A few compensations.

We aren't as judgmental as we used to be.
We're quicker to laugh, and not as eager to blame.
There's time left in this game. May we find
(Along with the inability to tell ourselves that
     we'll keep playing forever)
A few compensations.

Eight Basic Facts
about Memory

*T*he fact that people don't stop you when you ask them to stop
  you if you've told them this story
Doesn't mean that you haven't told it before.

The fact that you're only buying a couple of items at the store
Doesn't mean that you don't need to bring a list to the store.

The fact that you've put the passports in such a safe place that
  they couldn't possibly get lost
Doesn't mean that you actually, currently know where they are.

The fact that you've parked your car carefully
Doesn't mean, when the movie is over, that you will still recall
  where you parked the car.

The fact that you rushed upstairs because there was something you
  desperately needed in your closet
Doesn't mean, once you get there, that you'll recollect why
  you came.

The fact that you've known a person for thirty-five years
Doesn't mean, when you go to introduce him, that you can count on
  remembering his name.

The fact that you said good-bye and walked out the door
Doesn't mean that you won't be back immediately in order to get
  all the things you left behind.

And the fact that . . .
And the fact that . . .
And the fact that, the fact that, the fact that . . .

It's slipped my mind.

How Can People Want to Bring Children into This Terrible World?

(A POSSIBLE REPLY TO A POSSIBLE DAUGHTER-IN-LAW)

*E*verything good that once used to be wood is now plastic.
Whoever's in charge is either a crook or a creep.
And instead of from real human beings
We now get our money from money machines
And talk to each other after the sound of the beep.

But I still want a grandchild.

Going to lawyers can now cost us more than a Lear jet.
Going to bed can now give us a fatal disease.
A nuclear war, we've been told,
Will produce a nuclear winter so cold
That if we escape being roasted we're going to freeze.

But I still want a grandchild.

Terrorists blow us to pieces on foreign vacations.
Muggers and rapists attack us right on our own street.
And we're not even safe from harm
Locked up in our house with the burglar alarm
What with lead in our water and carcinogens in our meat.

But I still want a grandchild.

We've survived the decline and fall of the Roman Empire,
Endured Inquisitions, the Crash and the Second World War,
And lived through the Flood and the Plague.
So why don't you fertilize that egg
While I work on improving this planet a little bit more,

For my forthcoming grandchild.

FOREVER FIFTY

Before I Go

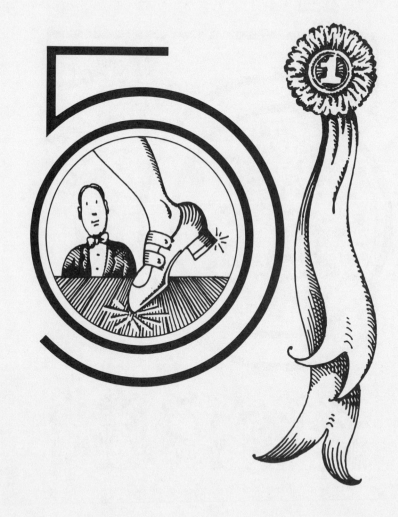

*B*efore I go, I'd like to have high cheekbones.
I'd like to talk less like New Jersey, and more like
    Claire Bloom.
And whenever I enter a room, I'd like an orchestra
    to burst into my theme song.
I'd like to have a theme song before I go.

Before I go, I'd like to learn to tap dance.
I'd like to play seven-card stud like a pro, not
    a dunce.
And I'd like Robert Redford, just once, to slide his
    fingers down my back from my neck to my waistline.
I'd like to have a waistline before I go.

Before I go, I'd like to win the door prize.
I'd like to be thought of as valiant and brilliant and
    thin.
And I'd like, when offered a choice between duty and sin,
    to not immediately choose duty.
I'd like a couple of offers before I go.

Before I go, I'd like to make things better.
I'd like to be told I've been more of a joy than
    a pain.
And I'd like those I love to know that they are the ones,
    if I could do it again, I'd do it with.
I'd like to do it again before I go.

You Might
As Well Laugh

So your ex-husband's much-younger wife is having a baby.
So your stockbroker says your best stock is down 42 points.
So your mother has broken her hip and your cute little grandson
      has just switched from Oreo cookies to joints,
And you need a new hot-water heater, and roof, immediately.

It's important to gaze without flinching at life's cruel afflictions.
It's important to let yourself grieve, but please don't overdo.
Remember that, given a choice between laughter and slashing your
      wrists with a razor,
You might as well laugh.

So you got a D-minus on your last physical checkup.
So the claims court has finished deciding your case, and you lose.
So your dog ran away and your cute little granddaughter just
      switched from pigtails to dyeing her hair chartreuse,
And your auto insurance has doubled—effective immediately.

It's useful to face the harsh facts and decline self-deception.
It's no good denying the truth, but do try to eschew
Dark thoughts. For given a choice between laughter and throwing
      yourself off a building,
You might as well laugh.

So you've disappointed your parents and failed all your children.
So nobody's tried to seduce you since '76.
So your hair's falling out, and your cute little father has just
      switched from Chaplin revivals to porno flicks,
And your orthodontist recommends braces—immediately.

It's mature to endure the full pain. But avoid thoughts of nooses.
And continue the trip in your ever-more-leaky canoe.
For given a choice between laughter and pistols or pills or
      carbon monoxide,
Or dumping a large dose of arsenic into your stew,
You might as well laugh.

Some Advice from a Mother to Her Married Son

The answer to do you love me isn't, I married you, didn't I?
Or, Can't we discuss this after the ballgame is through?
It isn't, Well that all depends on what you mean by "love."
Or even, Come to bed and I'll prove that I do.
The answer isn't, How can I talk about love when the
　　　bacon is burned and the house is an absolute mess
　　　and the children are screaming their heads off and
　　　I'm going to miss my bus?
The answer is yes.
The answer is yes.
The answer is yes.

When Asked to What They Owe the Success of Their Marriage, He and She Completely Agree that Love Is Accommodation

By six p.m. he's fainting from starvation.
She never thinks of food till nine at night.
They make a seven-thirty reservation—
He famished; she without an appetite.

He talks of cash flow and depreciation.
She talks of what is Beautiful and True.
And each endures the other's conversation
By gently nodding off until it's through.

They've different views of household decoration.
He loathes what she (and she what he) prefers.
But fair is fair. Their place of habitation
Holds tweedy armchairs (his), gilt cherubs (hers).

He wants to camp in forests on vacation.
She wants first-class hotels in Biarritz.
They therefore choose some compromise location
Midway between posh suites and snake-bite kits.

In bed they let no crazy wild sensation
Intrude upon their strict equality.
Instead, they work at joint gratification,
And work, and work, and work, relentlessly.

And comes their golden wedding celebration,
They'll praise each other for a job well done,
Agreeing, still, that love's accommodation,
But wishing that it could have been more fun.

Medical Tests

$\mathcal{M}$y periodontist thought that Ezio Pinza was a battle in
southern Italy.

My gastroenterologist couldn't tell Brian Donlevy from
Brian Aherne.

My dermatologist didn't know to whom I was referring when
I referred to Patti, Maxine and LaVerne.

My cardiologist thought that Little Sheba was a belly dancer
from Cairo.

My orthopedist was unaware that Allyson, Havoc and Haver were
three different Junes.

My urologist, when asked to hum the theme songs from "Let's
Pretend" and "Our Gal Sunday," wasn't familiar with either
the shows or the tunes.

My gynecologist thought that Gloria DeHaven was a retirement
community.

My physiotherapist couldn't tell Victor Mature from Victor
McLaglen or Vic Damone.

My ophthalmologist simply assumed that I was repeating myself
when I alluded to Simone Simon.

My endodontist thought that a Porfirio Rubirosa was a skin
rash.

My allergist, when pressed, could still not give the first and
last name of Jack Benny's wife.

My internist was incapable of singing "Mairzy Doats." It has
suddenly dawned on me

That I've put a bunch of kids in charge of my life.

More Questions

*F*ace lift, or no face lift—that is the question.
But I would like to mention fourteen others:
Are French-fried onion rings worth indigestion?
And why (although we vowed that we would never let this happen)
    have all us daughters turned into our mothers?
Will we, someday, grow unconcerned with fashion?
Is stoicism nicer than complaining?
Can reminiscence substitute for passion?
And how, now that we've saved our money for a rainy day,
    do we determine if—in fact—it's raining?
Is dyeing an improvement over graying?
Is marriage an impossible profession?
Is the inevitable worth delaying?
And when (although we know confession benefits the soul)
    is silence even better than confession?
Can someone really have too much insurance?
Should we expect our children to be grateful?
When is quitting wiser than endurance?
And when did we decide "mature" meant settling for a spoonful
    when what we all still crave is the whole plateful?

A Sexy
Old Lady

I'm intending to grow up to be a sexy old lady,
With a gleam in my eye and lace on my underpants.
Never vulgar, of course, but a perfumed and pedicured lady
Whose passions persist long long after the age of romance.

I'm intending to walk around town as a sexy old lady,
The kind that no Boy Scout need hurry to help cross the street.
With a light-hearted bounce that announces now here comes a lady
Who knows all the steps to the dance and has not lost the beat.

I'm intending to finish my days as a sexy old lady.
Yes, spiritual too—and compassionate, wise, mature, droll.
But along with that high-minded stuff I shall still be a lady
Aware of the joys that lie just slightly south of the soul.

I'm intending to go to my grave as a sexy old lady.
There'll be plenty of time for propriety after I'm dead.
So if heaven has answered my prayers,
I expect to be found, around eighty, upstairs
With my sexy old husband nestled beside me in bed.

The Pleasures of
an Ordinary Life

I've had my share of necessary losses,
Of dreams I know no longer can come true.
I'm done now with the whys and the becauses.
It's time to make things good, not just make do.
It's time to stop complaining and pursue
The pleasures of an ordinary life.

I used to rail against my compromises.
I yearned for the wild music, the swift race.
But happiness arrived in new disguises:
Sun lighting a child's hair. A friend's embrace.
Slow dancing in a safe and quiet place.
The pleasures of an ordinary life.

I'll have no trumpets, triumphs, trails of glory.
It seems the woman I've turned out to be
Is not the heroine of some grand story.
But I have learned to find the poetry
In what my hands can touch, my eyes can see.
The pleasures of an ordinary life.

Young fantasies of magic and of mystery
Are over. But they really can't compete
With all we've built together: A long history.
Connections that help render us complete.
Ties that hold and heal us. And the sweet,
Sweet pleasures of an ordinary life.